3/03   PEM

03. JUL 08

WITHDRAWN

Books should be returned or renewed by the
last date stamped above

J 709.04   GAFF, Jackie

20th Century Art

1920~40 . . . .

Awarded for excellence
to Arts & Libraries

PEMBURY

Kent
County
Council

20ᵀᴴ CENTURY ART

1920-40

REALISM & surrealism

A HISTORY OF MODERN ART

20TH CENTURY ART – 1920-40
was produced by

David West 👫 Children's Books

7 Princeton Court
55 Felsham Road
London SW15 1AZ

Picture Research: Brooks Krikler Research
Picture Editor: Carlotta Cooper

First published in Great Britain in 2000 by
Heinemann Library, Halley Court, Jordan Hill,
Oxford OX2 8EJ, a division of Reed Educational and
Professional Publishing Limited.

OXFORD MELBOURNE AUCKLAND
JOHANNESBURG BLANTYRE GABORONE
IBADAN PORTSMOUTH (NH) USA CHICAGO

04 03 02 01 00
10 9 8 7 6 5 4 3 2 1

ISBN 0 431 11602 4 (HB)
ISBN 0 431 11609 1 (PB)

British Library Cataloguing in Publication Data

Gaff, Jackie
1920-1940 Realism and surrealism. -
(Twentieth century art)
1. Art, Modern - 20th century - Juvenile literature
2. Surrealism - Juvenile literature 3. Realism in art -
Juvenile literature
I. Title
709' .04'063
Printed and bound in Italy

PHOTO CREDITS :
Abbreviations: t-top, m-middle, b-bottom, r-right, l-
left, c-centre.

Front cover & page 11 - Tate Publishing © Estate of
Stanley Spencer, all rights reserved, DACS 2000. 3, 4,
6 both, 7b, 8 both, 9b, 13t, 18, 19tr & b, 20t, 22r,
25b, 28 both & 29 - AKG London. 5t, 10b, 12t, 13b,
14 both, 15b, 16 both, 20b, 23b, 24b, 26t & 27 both-
Corbis. 5b - Tate Publishing © Salvador Dali -
Foundation Gala - Salvador Dali/DACS 2000. 7 & 9t -
Bridgeman Art Library © DACS 2000. 10t -
Bridgeman Art Library. 12b - Tate Publishing -
Reproduced by permission of the Henry Moore
Foundation. 15t - © Francis G. Mayer/Corbis. 17t -
Bridgeman Art Library © ARS, New York & DACS,
London 2000. 17b - © Philadelphia Museum of
Art/Corbis. 19tl - © Palace of Cortes, Cuernavaca,
Mexico, USA/Ian Marsell/Mexicolore/Bridgeman. 21 -
Tate Publishing © ADAGP, Paris & DACS London
2000. 22l - Bridgeman Art Library © ADAGP, Paris &
DACS London 2000. 23t - Corbis © ADAGP, Paris &
DACS London 2000. 24t - Bridgeman Art Library ©
Salvador Dali - Foundation Gala - Salvador
Dali/DACS 2000. 25t - Corbis © Salvidor Dali -
Foundation Gala - Salvidor Dali/DACS 2000. 26b -
Bridgeman Art Library © succession Picasso/DACS
2000

*The dates in brackets after a person's name
give the years that he or she lived.
The date that follows a painting's title and the
artist's name, gives the year it was painted.
'C.' stands for circa, meaning about or
approximately.*

*An explanation of difficult words can be
found in the glossary on page 30.*

20TH CENTURY ART
1920-40
REALISM & surrealism
A HISTORY OF MODERN ART

Jackie Gaff

Heinemann
LIBRARY

CONTENTS

THE RISE OF THE DICTATORS Economic problems in post-war Europe contributed to the coming to power of repressive absolute rulers, such as the Italian dictator Benito Mussolini. Nazism flourished in Germany under Adolf Hitler, while the Spanish Civil War of '36–'39 ushered in the dictatorship of General Francisco Franco, seen here in 1936 in Madrid.

THE CALL TO ORDER

The devastation of World War I sparked a profound desire for political and social change. The lessons of the past would be learnt – out of chaos would come order, a new world would be built from the rubble of the old.

In the arts, too, it was a time of re-assessment. The late 19th and early 20th century had seen radical changes, as first colour and then, with the development of abstract art, form were liberated from imitating the visible world of nature.

In the 1920s and '30s, artists reconsidered their relationship to the great art of the past and re-examined their role in modern society – could art be relevant to everyday life, and if so, how? Many painters and sculptors felt the time was ripe for a revival of the art style known as Realism, because of its focus on the down-to-earth realities of life and living.

Others headed off in completely the opposite direction – into the world of dreams and the unconscious. Known as the Surrealists, these artists set out to make the real unreal, the natural unnatural, and the ordinary utterly extraordinary!

FALLING ON HARD TIMES
Despite the desire for a better world, inflation and unemployment were rife in the '20s and '30s, as nations struggled to deal with the mountain of debts that had built up during the war years.

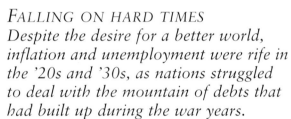

LOBSTER TELEPHONE, *Salvador Dalí, 1936*
One of the maddest of the Surrealists, Salvador Dalí (1904–89) also created some of the craziest sculptures and paintings. As in many Surrealist works, by pairing everyday but unlikely objects, he aimed to shock our senses and make us look at the world with fresh eyes.

THE BAUHAUS

At the forefront of the move to make art more relevant to everyday life was the Bauhaus, the German school of art, crafts and architecture founded in 1919 by the German-born architect Walter Gropius (1883–1969).

SCHOOL OF THOUGHT

Gropius aimed to break down the divisions between fine and applied art, and to forge closer links between art, society and industry – 'The designer must breathe a soul into the dead product of the machine,' he declared.

PRACTICAL DESIGN FOR LIVING
The Bauhaus pioneered the idea that form should follow function – that an object or building's appearance should be determined by its use or purpose. Shapes were simplified and decoration avoided, as in this Model B3 chair created in '25 by the Hungarian-born designer Marcel Breuer (1902–81).

NOTHING BUT THE BEST

Gropius recruited some of the finest avant-garde artists of his day to teach at the Bauhaus, including American Lyonel Feininger (1871–1956), Russian-born Vasily Kandinsky (1866–1944), German-Swiss Paul Klee (1879–1940) and Hungarian-born László Moholy-Nagy (1895–1946). Similar ideals to those of the Bauhaus were held by the De Stijl movement in the Netherlands and the Constructivists in Russia. All three also shared a belief in the purity and harmony of abstract art, and its importance in building a brave, new, post-war Europe.

THE GOLDEN FISH
PAUL KLEE, 1925

Klee was one of the most popular tutors at the Bauhaus, teaching the introductory design course as well as in the stained-glass and weaving workshops. Although great friends with Kandinsky, he kept apart from most other tutors in order to avoid the school's internal politics. Klee was an individual in more ways than one as, unlike the bulk of Bauhaus artists, his work was rarely totally abstract and always rooted in his love of nature. He described his art as 'taking a line for a walk', and his paintings are full of fantasy and childlike symbols and writing – reflecting the value he placed on the freshness of children's 'power to see' and his fascination for the scientific study of nature and the universe.

Paul Klee, photographed in 1921.

6

MOVING STORY

The avant-garde ideals of the Bauhaus placed them on the leftwing of politics, and the school's history was troubled. Although founded in Weimar, in southeastern Germany, it was forced to move on after a rightwing local government came to power and cut its funding. Next stop was Dessau, in '25, but seven years later the Dessau school was closed by the Nazis. The Bauhaus opened for a while in Berlin, but was finally shut down by the Nazis in '33. During the '30s many of the Bauhaus tutors emigrated to the USA.

Designed by Walter Gropius, the simple geometric form of the Bauhaus building in Dessau reflected the school's key principle of form following function.

NEW OBJECTIVITY

Not all German artists shared the Bauhaus school's belief in the need for abstract art to contribute towards building a better world. Others tended more towards criticism than construction, while their particular version of Realism was expressed through representational art.

REALITY OF THE TIMES

Although their styles varied, these German artists shared a detached and objective (as opposed to subjective) approach to their subjects. Because of this, the movement became known as Neue Sachlichkeit, which is German for 'new objectivity'. Its leading practitioners were Otto Dix (1891–1969) and George Grosz (1893–1959), both of whom were brutally critical of the corruption of post-war Germany.

Brecht's The Threepenny Opera *opened in Berlin in August '28.*

NIGHT AT THE OPERA

In musical plays such as *The Threepenny Opera*, the German-born playwright and poet Bertolt Brecht (1898–1956) tried to show how money perverts the rich and brutalizes the poor. Despite its attack on the corruption of post-war Germany, the opera was an instant hit – especially with the wealthy classes it satirized.

POLITICAL PAINTER
In this photograph taken in his studio in 1928, Grosz posed in front of his painting Pillars of Society *– two of his 'captains' of industry can be seen behind his shoulders. In '33, driven out by the worsening political situation in Germany, he emigrated to the USA.*

SOCIETY PORTRAITS

The political and economic situation was extremely unstable in Germany throughout the '20s and into the '30s, and while the poor suffered, others seemed to flaunt their wealth, power or decadent lifestyles. Grosz's vision was of 'mankind gone mad', and the chief targets for his bitingly savage caricatures were the fat cats depicted in his painting *Pillars of Society* ('26). These were the people he believed had either promoted or were profiting from the horrors of war – army officers, priests, and the capitalists who had made fortunes supplying weapons and other equipment.

PORTRAIT OF THE JOURNALIST
SYLVIA VON HARDEN
OTTO DIX, 1926

Dix, like Grosz, expressed his disgust at post-war Germany through acidic depictions of the atrocities of war and the decadence of bohemian life in Berlin, where the two artists lived – the 1972 film *Cabaret* also portrayed the city in their day, but presented a mellower picture. Among the targets for Dix's caustic style were the cynicism and sensuality of the period. To Dix, Sylvia von Harden's tough, androgynous appearance was the epitome of a world gone crazy.

Although persecuted by the Nazis, Dix was one of the few avant-garde artists who didn't leave Germany in the '30s.

STANLEY SPENCER

For some artists during the post-war years, their interest in Realism was grounded in their admiration for the great artists of the past. The avant-garde experiments of the 1900s and 1910s had shattered the traditions of Western painting and sculpture, and Realism was a way for artists to reconnect the art of the 20th century to its roots.

THE ARTIST AT WORK
Spencer was a superb draughtsman and began many of his paintings by planning and drawing the composition on paper. These drawings were then enlarged and transferred to the canvas, which Spencer painted using diluted and thinned oil paints and fine, sable-hair brushes.

A LIVING TRADITION

The chief historical inspiration for the British artist Stanley Spencer (1891–1959) were the religious masterpieces of the great Italian painter of the 13th and 14th centuries, Giotto di Bondone (1266/7–1337). Giotto was one of the first artists to break away from the thousand-year-old tradition in Western art of depicting static, stylized figures and scenes, and instead try to create the three-dimensional illusion of real life on a flat, two-dimensional surface.

A LIVING RELIGION

Like Giotto, Spencer wanted to depict Christianity as a living, breathing, everyday experience – Spencer said his aim was to make of 'the inmost of one's wishes, the most varied religious feelings…an ordinary fact of the street'. Spencer was born in the English village of Cookham, which he described as a 'holy suburb of Heaven', and spent most of his life there. In his religious paintings he retold the great stories of Christian history, setting them in the Cookham of his day and using the villagers as models.

MAN OF THE PEOPLE

Among Giotto's great achievements were the scenes from the lives of Christ and the Virgin Mary which he created on the walls of the Arena Chapel in Padua, in northeastern Italy. The painting opposite is from the Arena Chapel and shows the dead Christ after He was taken down from the Cross, in the Virgin's arms, surrounded by His mourning disciples. Unlike the stylized, emotionless figures that were the accepted convention of his day, the people in Giotto's painting are full of life and feeling.

THE LAMENTATION OF CHRIST, *Giotto, c. 1306*

THE HOLINESS OF LIFE

The warm humanity and childlike naivety of Spencer's style made him one of the most individual and important British artists of the 20th century. Although the bulk of his work lay in the retelling of religious stories, Spencer's sense of the holiness of life extended to the joy of simply being human. He expressed these feelings through paintings of nudes and of people going about their daily work, including a series of huge canvases showing the contribution towards the war effort made by shipbuilders on Scotland's River Clyde during World War II.

SAINT FRANCIS AND THE BIRDS
STANLEY SPENCER, 1935

St Francis of Assisi was born into a wealthy Italian family in about 1181, but abandoned all his belongings during his 20s for total poverty in imitation of Christ. He went on to found the Roman Catholic order of nuns and friars called the Franciscans. St Francis was also famous for his love of birds, which is why Spencer painted him surrounded by ducks and geese in a 20th-century Cookham farmyard. St Francis is wearing slippers and a green dressing-gown instead of his usual sandals and brown friar's habit in this painting, because Spencer based him on his ageing and slightly dotty father, William, who had taken to wandering about Cookham dressed in this way.

MOORE & HEPWORTH

Two other British artists who admired the great art of the past were the Yorkshire-born sculptors Henry Moore (1898–1986) and Barbara Hepworth (1903–1975).

12

RECUMBENT FIGURE
HENRY MOORE, 1938

Moore and Hepworth became famous for the holes they introduced to their sculptures in the early '30s. 'A hole can have as much meaning as a solid mass,' explained Moore, 'there is a mystery in a hole in a cliff or hillside, in its depth and shape.'

WORKING RELATIONSHIPS

Moore and Hepworth met after they began studying at the Leeds School of Art in 1919. They went out together for a short while, but their relationship soon became no more than a friendship. The two artists' studies continued in London, where Moore in particular was inspired by the ancient stone sculptures he saw at the British Museum. What he admired in this work was its emotional expressiveness and simplicity of form, as well as what he described as: 'Its "stoniness", by which I mean its truth to material, its tremendous power.'

Mayan chacmool, c. 10th–12th century

CARVED IN STONE

Among the art studied by Moore at London's British Museum were the sculptures known as chacmools. These carvings of reclining male gods were created by the Mayans, Toltecs and other early Mexican civilizations.

NATURAL CONNECTIONS

The work of Hepworth and Moore was also influenced by the natural world, from wind- and water-eroded hills and cliffs to bones, pebbles and shells – many of their sculptures were designed to be seen outdoors, in parks and public squares. Their early sculptures were carved directly into wood or stone, although in later years they created works that were cast in metals such as bronze.

MOTHER AND CHILD

Hepworth created this tender stone sculpture in '29, the year she had a son with her first husband, the sculptor John Skeaping (1901–80). Within a couple of years Hepworth's work had become totally abstract – it was to continue so for the remainder of her life.

13

THE REAL AMERICA

In the USA, a focus on Realism combined with the continuing push towards developing a distinctively American art, independent of European avant-garde movements. The artist Edward Hopper (1882–1967) summarized this tendency when he stated his own aims: 'Instead of subjectivity, a new objectivity. Instead of abstraction, a reaffirmation of representation… Instead of internationalism, an art based on the American scene.'

PHOTO-REALITY
One of the major Realists of the 20th century, Hopper spent most of his life in New York City. He made several visits to Europe in 1906–10, but remained unimpressed by European avant-garde art.

AMERICAN GOTHIC, *Grant Wood, 1930*

HOME TRUTHS
Wood used his sister and his dentist as models for the couple in this homage to the dignity of small-town life. The word 'Gothic' in the painting's title refers to the architectural style of the couple's simple white farmhouse.

AMERICAN TRADITION

Objective Realism had been part of the American art scene since the 1870s, when one of the foremost practitioners was Thomas Eakins (1844–1916). In the early 20th century, it was developed by the artists who came to be known as the Ashcan School because of their gritty depictions of everyday city life (in the USA, an ashcan is a dustbin). Leading Ashcan-ites included Robert Henri (1865–1929) and George Bellows (1882–1925), as well as Hopper.

TOWN AND COUNTRY

While artists such as Hopper homed in on the underbelly of big towns and cities, from the '30s onwards other Realists put their efforts into celebrating the quiet, hard-working lifestyles of rural and small-town Americans. This back-to-the-earth movement was named Regionalism, and its chief exponents included Grant Wood (1892–1942) and Thomas Hart Benton (1889–1975).

DEPRESSING REALITY
The collapse of the New York Stock Exchange in the Wall Street Crash of '29 ushered in a period of appalling hardship, first in the USA and then throughout the world. Regionalism was in part a reassertion of faith in the American way of life in the face of the national doubt raised by widespread economic depression.

14

NIGHTHAWKS, EDWARD HOPPER, 1942

Although physically set in the USA of his day, Hopper's haunting paintings go far beyond their period, to depict timeless truths about the loneliness and desolation of life in big cities and towns.

Many of Hopper's works have no people in them at all. When, as in *Nighthawks*, there are people, the feeling of loneliness persists – these four New Yorkers in a late-night diner are together, yet somehow apart.

Queues for food handouts were a common sight in the '30s.

GEORGIA O'KEEFFE

Realism was not the only route for American artists during the '20s and '30s. The work of Georgia O'Keeffe (1887–1986) moved between representation and abstraction, but even in her most naturalistic paintings, making her subjects true to life was never her primary concern.

HIDDEN TRUTHS

Instead, influenced by the ideas of the Russian-born pioneer of abstract art Vasily Kandinsky, O'Keeffe wanted to express the essential truths that lie beneath surface appearances. 'Nothing is less real than realism…' stated O'Keeffe, 'It is only by selection, by elimination, by emphasis that we get at the real meaning of things.'

16

MODERN MUSEUM Founded in '29, New York's Museum of Modern Art (MoMA) today holds the largest and finest modern art collection in the world. In '46, O'Keeffe became the first woman artist to be honoured with a major exhibition of her work at MoMA.

MODERN LOVE STORY

O'Keeffe's career took off after some abstract drawings were shown to the influential photographer and gallery owner, Alfred Stieglitz (1864–1946). Stieglitz liked the drawings so much that he gave O'Keeffe her first one-woman show in 1917, and O'Keeffe and Stieglitz liked each other so much that they married in '24.

COW'S SKULL WITH CALICO ROSES
GEORGIA O'KEEFFE, 1932

Begun in the early '30s, O'Keeffe's paintings of cow's skulls are among her most representational works. Artificial flowers are used in funerals by some New Mexicans, and for many people, the skull is also a symbol of death. For O'Keeffe, though, it seems to have stood for life – she said she had used 'the beautiful white bones' she had found in the desert 'to say what is to me the wideness and wonder of the world as I live in it.'

Married to a photographer, O'Keeffe was one of the most photographed women of her day.

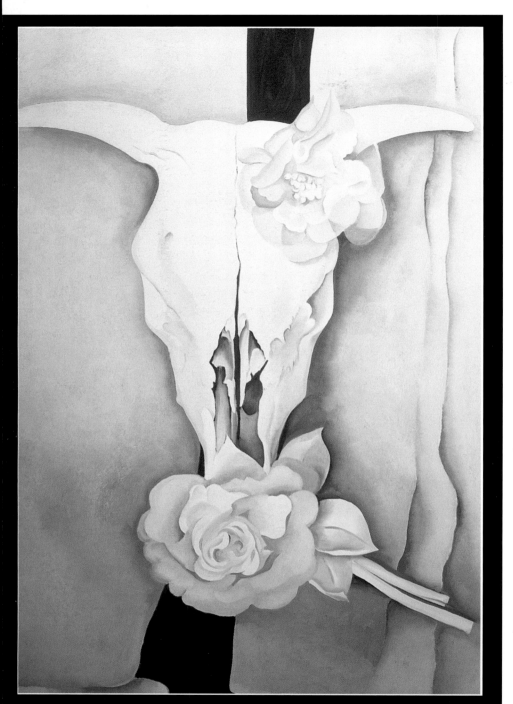

IN LOVE WITH THE LANDSCAPE

The pair lived in New York for much of the '20s, but in '29 O'Keeffe revisited her second great love – the dramatic desert landscape of the southwestern State of New Mexico. From then on, O'Keeffe divided her year mainly between New York, where Stieglitz lived, and New Mexico, moving there permanently a few years after his death in '46. The deep blue sky and the yellows, oranges, reds and purples of the sand hills of the New Mexican desert, together with the bleached bones and skulls she found there, were to remain O'Keeffe's chief inspiration for much of the rest of her life.

PAYING PRECISE ATTENTION TO DETAIL

In the '20s, O'Keeffe painted a number of New York scenes that are often described as Precisionist. This was an American art style which, influenced by photography and the fragmentation of Cubism, celebrated objects and industrial landscapes in a very clear-cut, exact way. Besides O'Keeffe, leading Precisionists included Charles Demuth (1883–1935) and Charles Sheeler (1883–1965).

LANCASTER, *Charles Demuth, 1920*

MEXICAN MURALISTS

Another branch of Realism developed in Mexico, south of the US border, during the '20s. In their series of vast wall paintings, the Mexican muralists Diego Rivera (1886–1957), José Clemente Orozco (1883–1949) and David Alfaro Siqueiros (1896–1974) founded the first major modern art movement to originate outside Europe.

LEANING TO THE LEFT

All three artists were committed leftwingers, and their work was funded by Mexico's new socialist government. Led by the art-loving President Alvaro Obregón, this was set up at the end of the 1910s, after the country's dictator, Porfirio Díaz, was overthrown by a revolution.

BIG PERSONALITY Rivera was a larger-than-life character, in more ways than one.

18

SLAVERY IN THE SUGAR PLANTATION
DIEGO RIVERA, 1930–31

This striking painting is part of a huge, 4-by-32-metre mural on the walls of the Palace of Cortez, in the Mexican town of Cuernavaca. The palace had been built by Hernan Cortez, the leader of the Spanish invaders who conquered the Aztecs in 1519–21, and for Rivera, the mural was an opportunity to turn a symbol of defeat into a memorial to colonial oppression.

Rivera had lived in Paris during the 1910s, where he had experimented with Cubism. The major influence on his mural style, however, was the visit he and Siqueiros made to Italy in 1919, where they were both overwhelmed by the magnificent wall paintings created by Giotto and the great Italian masters who followed him, in the 14th and 15th centuries.

THE WRITING ON THE WALL

Obregón turned the walls of Mexico's
schools, hospitals and other public buildings
over to Rivera, Orozco and Siqueiros,
encouraging them to educate and inspire
their fellow Mexicans by painting the story
of their country's oppressed past and what
everyone hoped would be a prosperous
future. Although their individual styles
varied, all three artists drew upon Mexican
folk art and the art of their ancestors, the
Mayans and the Aztecs.

ROCKY TIMES WITH THE ROCKEFELLERS

Rivera worked in the USA in the early '30s,
and in '33 was commissioned to create a mural
for the Rockefeller Center, New York. This
was surprising, since Rivera was a Communist,
while the Rockefellers were the world's richest
oil family and leaders of Western capitalism.
Things went fairly well until the Rockefellers
realized that the mural included a portrait of
Lenin, the founder of Russian Communism.
The project was cancelled, Rivera was paid off,
and his half-finished mural was chiselled from
the walls. The painting right is of the mural's
pilot-like central character and is taken from
Rivera's recreation of the Rockefeller mural,
done after his return to Mexico in '34.

MAN, CONTROLLER OF THE UNIVERSE, *Diego Rivera, 1934*

SUPER-REALITY

Back in Europe during the '20s, writers and artists were exploring an alternative reality to that of the everyday world. By setting free the unconscious mind and the world of dreams, they aimed to create a kind of heightened, super-reality – in French, *sur* means 'above', and the movement was known as Surrealism.

Breton came to be regarded as the 'Pope of Surrealism'.

DEAD END OF DADA

Surrealism was launched in Paris in '24 by the French poet and critic André Breton (1896–1966). It grew out of the anti-art movement Dada, which had run out of steam by the early '20s – Breton said that Dada had opened 'wide the doors, but…they opened on to a corridor which was leading nowhere'. The Surrealists took what they believed to be the best of Dada – its shock tactics and love of nonsense and illogicality – and channelled them into new forms of creativity.

CREATIVE ACCIDENTS

Breton was a great believer in tapping into his unconscious via trance-like automatism, defining this as 'the absence of any control exercised by reason'. A number of Surrealist artists, including Max Ernst (1891–1976), also tried to let ideas and images develop by chance, without conscious control – they called the process automatic drawing.

IN YOUR DREAMS

Another key influence was psychology, the science of the mind. The Surrealists were hugely interested in the research of the Austrian psychoanalyst Sigmund Freud (1856–1939) into the meaning of dreams, and the clues they can give to our unconscious thoughts and desires.

THE IMPORTANCE OF BEING ERNST
Surrealism started off as a literary movement, and German-born Max Ernst was one of the first artists to explore it. Ernst had been one of the leaders of German Dadaism, but he had met Breton in '21 and settled in Paris a year later.

20

FOREST AND DOVE
MAX ERNST, 1927

Ernst invented forms of automatic painting that were a bit like brass
rubbing. One involved rubbing with a pencil or charcoal on paper laid
over a rough surface – he called this 'frottage' (from *frotter*, French for 'to
rub'). Ernst called the technique he used for the background of *Forest and
Dove* 'grattage' (from *gratter*, meaning 'to scratch') – here, he laid a
thickly painted, but still wet canvas on top of fish bones and pieces of
wood, and then scraped at the paint. After beginning the painting in this
way, Ernst's imagination took over to create a lonely bird trapped inside a
cage, a prisoner in a nightmarish forest of looming, threatening trees.

21

INTERNATIONAL SURREALISM

In unlocking the unconscious, Surrealism was less of an art style than an attitude of mind, and the paintings and sculptures of individual artists vary enormously.

So, just as no two people dream the same dream, the paintings of Max Ernst, René Magritte (1898–1967) and Joan Miró (1893–1983) all look very different from one another.

TIME TRANSFIXED
RENÉ MAGRITTE, 1938

A toy-sized steam train puffs out of a fireplace – Magritte's style was meticulously realistic but his imagery was totally unreal. In other paintings, he turned clouds into loaves of French bread, and rain into suited men in bowler hats. In making the real unreal, and the ordinary strange, his work was always startling and often shocking or disturbing.

A man in a bowler hat first appeared in Magritte's paintings during the '30s, sometimes as a self-portrait. Magritte also posed for photographs dressed up in this outfit, as he did here in '67.

NO PLACE LIKE HOME

Surrealism attracted artists of many nationalities, some of them based in Paris, but others living and working outside France. Magritte, for example, was born in Belgium and lived there most of his life, apart from a brief spell in Paris during the '20s. Miró was a Spaniard, who until the mid-'30s divided his year between Paris and his family's farm at Montroig, near Barcelona.

WORLD OF TALENT

Other leading Surrealists included Frenchmen Hans Arp (1887–1966) and André Masson (1896–1987), French-born Americans Yves Tanguy (1900–55) and Marcel Duchamp (1887–1968), American Man Ray (1890–1977), Matta (*b.* 1911) of Chile, German-Swiss Meret Oppenheim (1913–85), British-born Mexican Leonora Carrington (*b.* 1917) and the Spaniard Salvador Dalí (1904–89).

RANGE OF INTERESTS

For some artists Surrealism was a phase they went through, but for many it was their life's work. And that work covered a wide range of art forms, from poetry and prose, to painting, sculpture, photography and film-making. Miró was a painter, sculptor, designer and ceramicist, for instance, while Magritte painted and sculpted, as well as making films.

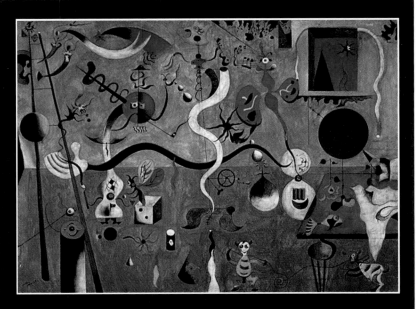

HARLEQUIN'S CARNIVAL
JOAN MIRÓ, 1924–25

Miró was one of a few Surrealists whose work tended towards abstraction. His paintings are full of bizarre shapes, many of which look like animals or microscopic organisms. Strange insect-like creatures dance and make music in *Harlequin's Carnival*, for example, while an ear is fixed to the top of the ladder on the left. Miró said that the painting was inspired by 'hallucinations brought on by hunger'. This kind of abstraction is known as biomorphic, because the forms are based on organic, rather than geometric, shapes.

Miró was living mainly on the island of Majorca by the time this photograph was taken in the '70s.

23

SALVADOR DALI

The most famous – and most infamous – Surrealist of all was the Spaniard Salvador Dalí. He joined the movement in '29, and was expelled ten years later. This was partly because he was getting too big for his boots, but also because Breton objected to Dalí's rightwing political views and felt that his style was becoming more traditional.

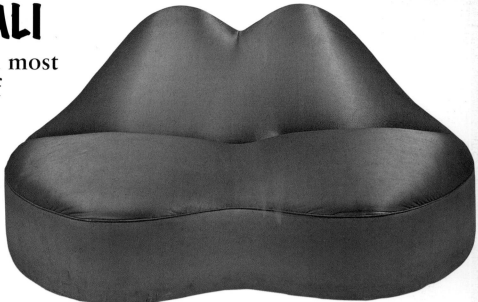

MAE WEST LIPS SOFA, *Salvador Dalí, 1936–37*
Dalí was the height of fashion in the '30s in more ways than one. As well as this tribute to the film star Mae West, he created surreal hats, bags and jewellery for the fashion guru Elsa Schiaparelli.

24

TREADING THE LIGHT FANTASTIC
Among the many outlets for Dalí's creative energy was set design for modern ballets. These included *Bacchanale*, which opened in New York in '39, and *Ballet of Gala*, which premiered in Venice in '61 – Gala was the name of Dalí's wife.

A gigantic eye with a clock as its pupil dominated Dalí's set designs for Ballet of Gala ('61).

ALL THE WORLD'S A STAGE

Dalí was a master at promoting himself and his work, often through outrageous stunts – in '36, for instance, he gave a lecture wearing a diving suit, and nearly suffocated. As a result, he rapidly became extremely fashionable and extremely rich, prompting Breton to nickname him 'Avida Dollars' (an anagram of Salvador Dalí).

MINE OF CREATIVITY

Above all, Dalí was wildly inventive, with passion for everything from painting and sculpture, to fashion design, writing and film-making – he co-wrote the first Surrealist film, the macabre *Un Chien Andalou* ('28), with the Spanish director Luis Buñuel (1900–83). Dalí's work was sometimes hilariously funny, but more often than not it was full of terror and violence. 'The only difference between me and a madman is that I am not mad,' he once said, and the majority of his paintings are nightmare visions of a drooping, melting, rotting world.

APPARITION OF FACE AND FRUIT DISH ON A BEACH
SALVADOR DALÍ, 1938

Dalí described his paintings as 'hand-painted dream photographs', and no matter how fantastical his imagery, his style was always photographically realistic. He often played the kind of visual trick shown in this work, making pictures that portray more than one thing at once. Here a ghostly face dissolves into a tall glass dish of fruit, on a beach which folds down on the right, like a tablecloth. The nose, mouth and chin of the face are also the back of a seated woman, while the landscape towards the top is also a dog – its head faces to the right, and its collar is a bridge.

Dalí's wife Gala (c. 1884–1982) was his manager and his muse – she's the one in the fencing mask in this early '40s photo of the famous pair.

PICASSO'S *GUERNICA*

Whether or not Dalí was mad may have been open to question – that the world was going mad during the '30s seemed certain. While Hitler and Mussolini grew ever more powerful in Germany and Italy, Spain was torn apart by the civil war between Franco's rightwing Nationalists and his opponents, the Republicans.

THE MADNESS OF WAR

On 26 April 1937, acting as Franco's allies, the Nazis bombed and virtually destroyed the northern Spanish town of Guernica. This atrocious act shocked the world and spurred the creation of one of its most devastating condemnations of violence – the painting *Guernica*, by the great Spanish artist Pablo Picasso (1881–1973).

BAITING THE BULL
Two of the dominant images in Guernica, *the bull and the horse, were inspired by the national sport of Spain, bullfighting. Picasso was passionate about it, attending bullfights whenever he could and celebrating them in a number of paintings.*

26

REPUBLICAN SYMPATHIES

Picasso was living in Paris when the Spanish Civil War broke out in '36. As a supporter of the Republicans, he was asked by them to make something for the Spanish Pavilion at the Paris International Exhibition, which was to open in July '37. He was planning this work when news of the bombing of Guernica reached him and inspired him to create a totally different painting.

THE LONG JOURNEY HOME

Picasso didn't want *Guernica* to be shown in Spain while Franco was in power. It was shipped to New York's Museum of Modern Art in the late '30s, and it wasn't until '81 that the painting reached the Prado museum in the Spanish capital, Madrid – eight years after Picasso's death and six years after Franco's.

Republican troops prepare for an attack.

A NATION AT WAR, A PEOPLE DIVIDED

The Spanish Civil War was the climax of a struggle between the supporters and opponents of the Republican government set up in '31 to replace the rule of King Alfonso XIII. Fighting broke out in '36 and ended three years later, after the death of tens of thousands of soldiers and civilians, with the Nationalists' capture of the capital, Madrid. General Franco ruled Spain as a dictator until his death in '75.

GUERNICA
PABLO PICASSO, 1937

Painted entirely in black, grey and white, *Guernica* is huge – roughly 3.5 by 7.8 metres. The painting went far beyond the specific event of the town's bombing, to symbolize the madness, terror and suffering of all war, through its broken, distorted animals and people. At its heart is the screaming horse, which Picasso said represented the people, while the bull to its left stood for 'brutality and darkness'.

DEATH AND DESTRUCTION
The Nazis bombed Guernica for four hours, destroying 70 per cent of the town's buildings and killing more than 1,000 of its 7,000 citizens.

THE ART OF REPRESSION

Politics played a far more active role than simply inspiring great works like *Guernica* during the '30s. In Germany and the USSR, politicians tried to enforce the art styles that they felt best served their political beliefs.

OUT WITH THE NEW, IN WITH THE OLD

Hitler came to power in Germany in '33, while Joseph Stalin was virtual dictator of the USSR from the late '20s until his death in '53. Both men knew how useful art could be as propaganda. They also knew what they did and didn't like – avant-garde was out, and classical or traditional Realism was in.

DEGENERATE ART

The Nazis labelled modern art 'degenerate' (meaning 'corrupt' or 'degrading') and their campaign against it included exhibitions intended to ridicule avant-garde artists and their work. The climax was the Munich Degenerate Art Exhibition of '37, which featured works by over 100 artists, including Ernst, Grosz, Klee and Picasso.

The Beach *(1921) by the leading German artist Max Beckmann (1884–1950) was included in the Degenerate Art Exhibition of '37.*

WORKER AND COLLECTIVE FARM WOMAN, *Vera Mukhina, 1936 This 25-metre high statue of idealized workers towered above visitors to the Soviet pavilion at the 1937 Paris International Exhibition.*

28

WHISTLE WHILE YOU WORK

This Realism wasn't to be used for the kind of social criticism practised by George Grosz and Otto Dix, though. Instead, it was put to work churning out idealized, chocolate-box portraits of musclebound workers and supposedly happy German and Soviet families.

The work of artists who didn't toe the line was banned from museums and art galleries or destroyed. As for the artists themselves, some were persecuted – the ones who upset Stalin were packed off to Siberian labour camps – while others either went into hiding or chose to emigrate, with most opting for the USA.

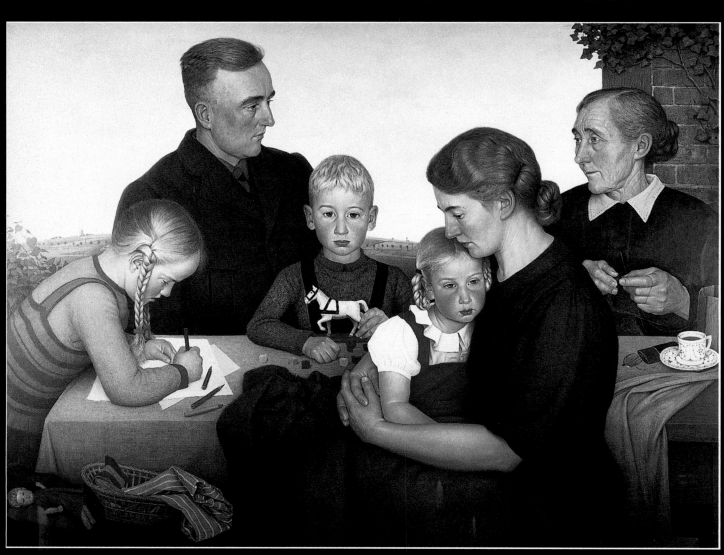

KAHLENBERG FARMER'S FAMILY
ADOLF WISSEL, 1939

Hitler's persecution of the Jews was founded in his belief in the superiority of the Aryan race of north Europe – of which Germans were, he thought, the purest example.

In Nazi Germany, artists were encouraged to promote this doctrine of racial superiority through romantic images of 'pure-blooded' German families at work and at play.

GLOSSARY

ABSTRACT ART Art that does not attempt to represent the real world, but which instead expresses meaning or emotion through shapes and colours.

BAUHAUS, THE A German school of art, crafts and architecture of 1919–33, which was hugely influential in forging links between art, design and industry.

CONSTRUCTIVISM A Russian, geometric abstract art movement that developed just before the Revolution of 1917. Artists used industrial materials and tried to break down the gap between fine and applied art.

CUBISM An art style founded by Pablo Picasso and Georges Braque in 1907. Cubist works fragmented the subject into geometric shapes and presented several viewpoints at once.

DADA An anti-sense and anti-tradition movement in art and literature born in Europe and the USA during World War I.

DE STIJL A Dutch, geometric abstract art magazine and movement founded in 1917, which aimed to apply laws of universal harmony to art, life and society.

NEUE SACHLICHKEIT German for 'new objectivity' – a German art movement of the 1920s and early '30s, in which artists used a Realist style for savage criticisms of post-war German society.

PRECISIONISM An American art movement that began in about 1915, in which objects and industrial scenes were depicted in a very clear-cut, sharply defined way.

REALISM A traditional style of art that attempts to give an unidealized view of ordinary, everyday life, often to make a social or political point.

REGIONALISM An American art movement of the 1930s and '40s, in which artists used a Realist style to celebrate rural and small-town life in the USA.

REPRESENTATIONAL ART Art that portrays things seen in the real world. Also known as figurative art.

SURREALISM A movement in art and literature that grew out of Dada in the early '20s. Fascinated by the world of dreams and the unconscious, Surrealists made the real unreal, and the everyday disturbing and strange.

30

WORLD EVENTS

- USA: women over 21 get vote
- Chinese communist party founded
- Russia becomes USSR
- Italy: Mussolini seizes power
- Britain: first Labour government elected
- Iran: Reza Khan rules as shah
- Britain: General Strike
- German stock market collapses
- USSR: Stalin's first five-year plan
- USA: Wall Street Crash; Hoover elected president
- India: Gandhi leads Salt March protest
- Japanese army occupies Chinese Manchuria
- Nazis take control of Reichstag (parliament)
- Hitler in power, as Chancellor of Germany
- China: Communists led by Mao on Long March
- Italy invades Abyssinia (Ethiopia)
- Spanish Civil War begins
- Edward VIII abdicates
- India: Congress Party wins elections
- Germany & Austria unite (Anschluss)
- Spanish Civil War ends
- Start of World War II

TIMELINE

	ART	DESIGN	THEATRE & FILM	BOOKS & MUSIC
20	•*Canadian Group of Seven formed*	•*London: Edwin Lutyens' Cenotaph in Whitehall*	•*Eugene O'Neill:* Beyond the Horizon	•*Edith Wharton:* The Age of Innocence
21	•*Max Ernst's Surrealist* Elephant of Celebes	•*Germany: E. Mendelsohn's sculptural Einstein Tower*	•*Rudolph Valentino stars in* The Sheik	•*D.H. Lawrence:* Women in Love
22	•*Picasso's Neoclassical* Women on the Beach	•*De Stijl founder Theo van Doesburg lectures at Bauhaus*	•*F.W. Murnau's chilling* Nosferatu	•*James Joyce:* Ulysses •*T.S. Eliot:* The Waste Land
23	•*Duchamp:* The Bride Stripped Bare	•*Le Corbusier's* Towards a New Architecture *published*	•*George Bernard Shaw:* Saint Joan	•*W.B. Yeats wins Nobel Prize for Literature*
24	•*Paris: Breton's first Surrealist manifesto*	•*Netherlands: Gerrit Rietveld's Schröder House*	•*S. O'Casey:* Juno & the Paycock •*MGM formed*	•*Gershwin:* Rhapsody in Blue •*E.M. Forster:* Passage to India
25	•*Paris: first Surrealist exhibition*	•*Paris: Art Deco celebrated at international exhibition*	•*Sergei Eisenstein:* The Battleship Potemkin	•*Franz Kafka:* The Trial •*Alban Berg's opera* Wozzeck
26	•*Grosz:* Pillars of Society •*Death of Claude Monet*	•*Bauhaus designer Marcel Breuer's Model B3 chair*	•*Fritz Lang's futuristic* Metropolis	•*A. Gide:* The Counterfeiters •*A.A. Milne:* Winnie-the-Pooh
27	•*Ernst's frottage:* Forest and Dove	•*USA: Buckminster Fuller's futuristic Dymaxion House*	•*First successful 'talkie',* The Jazz Singer	•*Kern & Hammerstein's hit musical* Show Boat
28	•*Demuth:* I Saw the Figure 5 in Gold	•*USA: van Alen's Art Deco Chrysler Building (to '30)*	•*Buñuel & Dalí's Surrealist film* Un Chien Andalou	•*Bertolt Brecht's* The Threepenny Opera
29	•*New York: founding of MoMA*	•*France: Le Corbusier's Cubist Villa Savoye (to '31)*	•*Academy Awards:* Broadway Melody *wins 'Best Picture'*	•*Virginia Woolf:* A Room of One's Own
30	•*Grant Wood:* American Gothic	•*Britain: Lutyen's Castle Drogo (from '10)*	•*Dietrich in* The Blue Angel •*Noël Coward:* Private Lives	•*Dashiell Hammett:* The Maltese Falcon
31	•*Rivera completes murals in Palace of Cortez*	•*New York: Empire State Building completed*	•*Cagney in* Public Enemy •*Bela Lugosi in* Dracula	•*Deaths of Nellie Melba & Kahlil Gilbran*
32	•*O'Keeffe:* Cow's Skull with Calico Roses	•*Britain: Anglepoise lamp designed by G. Carwardine*	•*Johnny Weissmuller in* Tarzan, the Ape Man	•*A. Huxley:* Brave New World •*Cole Porter:* 'Night & Day'
33	•*Germany: suppression of 'degenerate art' begins*	•*Berlin: Bauhaus School closed by Nazis*	•*Fay Wray in* King Kong •*Marx Brothers:* Duck Soup	•*Erskine Caldwell:* God's Little Acre
34	•*USA: 'The Machine' exhibition at MoMA*	•*Britain: Wells Coates' Bakelite Ekco AD65 radio*	•*Shirley Temple (aged 6) a star after* Stand Up & Cheer	•*S. Rachmaninov:* Rhapsody on a Theme of Paganini
35	•*Spencer:* Saint Francis and the Birds	•*USA: Raymond Loewy's streamlined Coldspot fridge*	•*Fred Astaire & Ginger Rogers star in* Top Hat	•*Benny Goodman is 'King of Swing'*
36	•*London: International Surrealist Exhibition*	•*Germany: Volkswagen Beetle designed by F. Porsche*	•*Charlie Chaplin stars in* Modern Times	•*Spanish poet F. García Lorca executed in Civil War*
37	•*Picasso responds to Nazi bombing, with* Guernica	•*USA: Frank Lloyd Wright's Falling Water (to '39)*	•*Disney:* Snow White •*Jean Renoir:* Grande Illusion	•*Agatha Christie:* Death on the Nile
38	•*Moore:* Recumbent Figure •*Magritte:* Time Transfixed	•*Finland: Alvar Aalto's Villa Mairea (to '41)*	•*Hitchcock:* The Lady Vanishes •*Thorton Wilder:* Our Town	•*Jean-Paul Sartre:* Nausea •*D. du Maurier:* Rebecca
39	•*Dalí expelled from Surrealist movement*	•*Futuristic designs shown at New York World's Fair*	•*Release of* The Wizard of Oz & Gone With the Wind	•*John Steinbeck:* The Grapes of Wrath

INDEX